Bob Dylan
Through the Eyes of Joe Alper

Visit www.dylanbook.com to blog about the book,
help identify those who are not yet identified, correct or contribute, and
generally reminisce about the times gone by that have indeed changed.

Please address all inquiries to info@dylanbook.com.

Printed and bound in the U.S.A.

ISBN # 978-0-9800463-0-4

Mixed Sources
Product group from well-managed
forests and other controlled sources
www.fsc.org Cert no. SCS-COC-001090
© 1996 Forest Stewardship Council
FSC

It's the start of 1962. You're at home, and you're not quite four years old, and your parents make just enough money to get by. In walks a young guy dressed in a flannel shirt and carrying a guitar, visiting from Manhattan. But you don't live in Coney Island and your father isn't Woody Guthrie; and you haven't grown up seeing older men, nearly your father's age, crowded in the parlor, dressed in flannel shirts, tuning, tuning, tuning, playing, singing and tuning some more. No. You live in Schenectady and your father is an artist with a camera.

Your parents, being decent and charitable, invite the guy to stay over with his girlfriend, and have assured him that he should count on staying whenever he played his songs at one of the local coffee shops. You might have been wondering who this fellow is, but it doesn't really matter: he and his girlfriend are nice and friendly, and they sit down on the floor to play with you and your sister, building a tower out of your blocks (or maybe it's a strange elevated little throne?), and the stranger makes a funny face that makes you laugh and gets you to point. You've never seen THAT face before – look at that, he's the one, he's the one, look at that, he he hehehehaha.

George Alper was lucky to have the parents he did; and his father, Joe, was lucky to have already met up with the young Bob Dylan. In early May, 1961, after he'd been in New York less than four months, Dylan headed with some friends to Branford, Connecticut, on Long Island Sound, to play a folk music festival at the old Montowese Hotel, which was said to have been Mark Twain's very favorite summer resort. Dylan was still scuffling: although he had just completed his first extended paid gig at Gerde's Folk City, as the opening act for John Lee Hooker, he was about to be turned down for record deals by Folkways Records, Vanguard, and Elektra. Right at that moment, Dylan was standing at what his friends in Minneapolis would call the crossroads, the same mystical placeless place where Robert Johnson was supposed to have sold his soul to the devil thirty years earlier in order to become a musical genius. It was the only way Dylan's friends could explain why, when he returned to Minneapolis for a short visit later that spring, Dylan was singing and playing like he never had in his Dinkytown days, an astonishing leap ahead in so short a time.

Joe Alper was there with his camera at the crossroads in Branford, and he took some of the very first pictures of Bob Dylan truly becoming himself. Alper later took pictures of Dylan alone with his guitar in Schenectady in what look like promotional poses, and then some pictures of him playing at Gerde's -- the very same performance which the critic Robert Shelton would soon write up in the rave review for *The New York Times* that gave the performer his first taste of fame outside the little folksingers' circle in Greenwich Village.

Alper naturally took pictures again when Dylan traveled north the following January to play at Caffé Lena in Saratoga and the San Remo in Schenectady, and stayed over at the Alpers' home on Brandywine Avenue nearby. Here was Bob Dylan becoming yet another Bob Dylan -- the one who would appear in the pictures Alper took late in April 1962, at the first recording session for what would become *The Freewheelin' Bob Dylan*, with Dylan wearing the eyeglasses he did not wear on stage, clip-on shades covering the lenses.

In *Chronicles: Volume One*, Dylan writes that a tidal wave broke over his world during these weeks and months in 1961 and in early 1962. There were more tremors and tidal waves to come, some of them at Newport, Rhode Island during the summers of 1964 and 1965. Joe Alper was there then, too, snapping.

You can look at these pictures and see the progress of two artists.

You look at them and find evidence of Dylan as the shapechanger Liam Clancy has said he was, assuming, for an instant, in 1962, shapes he would show the world three years later -- and then returning just as quickly to his younger, baby-fat-cheeked self.

You can look on these pictures as historic, if only because the photographs taken on September 26, 1961, and April 24, 1962, and July 25, 1965, captured landmark events in Dylan's early career. (Just having those pictures on your shelf is worth whatever price it is you're being asked for to pay for this book.)

You can look on these pictures as historic in another way, too, especially the off-stage pictures taken at the Alpers' or at Gil Turner's wedding (notice the great Reverend Gary Davis either deep in listening or nodding off), capturing a time before the flood or the plague or whatever image you prefer swept over the country in the later 1960s -- a time just before that, inside the folk music paradise that Dylan now says he had to leave, like Adam left the garden.

And after you have looked at all of Joe Alper's pictures, I have a feeling that you'll flip back to linger over the one of Jeri Alper and Suze Rotolo, and of gleeful little George pointing over the blocks at the guy in the flannel shirt, who in that instant seemed to be Harpo Marx.

--Sean Wilentz
  Christmas Day, 2007

For Benjamin, Joe, Jeri, and Jackie

I was a few months shy of four years old when Bob Dylan first came to stay at our home in Schenectady, NY. The year was 1961, and, of course, my memories of his visit are dim at best. I do remember playing with him and Suze Rotolo, his girlfriend at the time. I remember anyone who ever took the time to play with me when I was a kid. But memory is a tricky thing; even eyewitness testimony is now regularly called into question by experts. My memories of Dylan are necessarily influenced by the photographic record my father created over the course of four years. But there are things I remember which have no photographic documentary counterpart. I remember falling asleep to Dylan's music on the cot in the back room which passed for a dressing room at *Caffe Lena* in Saratoga, NY while the rest of my family sat and listened. I remember standing in front of my dad at the enlarger in the basement of our second floor flat. The amber-tinted safelight illuminated the darkroom, and I stood between my dad and the counter that held the enlarger and easel which framed the negatively displayed images on the photographic paper. Dad would let me step on the foot pedal which triggered the exposure of the print, and I watched- amazed every time- as he dipped the paper into the developer and the images revealed themselves after a couple of minutes. I suppose my early, accidental indoctrination into photography ingrained itself into my brain and eventually led me to pursue the vocation myself. Some people worry about becoming their parents; I embrace it.

Joe

The years went by, and Dylan stopped staying with us as his star rose and his trips to upstate New York ceased. Dad died from kidney failure after battling polycystic kidney disease for years, and my sisters moved out, leaving Mom and me at home. I remember trading looks of confusion with Mom in 1969, when we first played the copy of *Nashville Skyline* sent to us by the record company. "He must have damaged his vocal chords in the motorcycle accident," she speculated. Other than the occasional call from a record company or writer requesting permission to use one of Dad's photos in an upcoming project, that pretty much closes the book on my memories of Dylan.

I don't recall talking too much about Dylan and his connection with our family again until just recently. Friends I have known since the '70s were quite surprised when I told them about the project to put my dad's images together in a collection for publication. "Dylan stayed at your house?" Most were astounded. Some were downright disbelieving. Even in college, as my roommate played "Tangled Up in Blue" and the rest of *Blood on the Tracks* incessantly, I didn't mention my passing connection to Dylan. I suppose it didn't seem like a very big deal to me, and I can only theorize that my personal contact with him kept me from placing him on a pedestal. How can you idolize a guy you showed how to use building blocks when you were three?

Here then, are the best of Joe's Bob Dylan photos. Those taken in unguarded moments capture the essence of Dylan without intruding. As for Joe's concert photography, it speaks for itself. Enjoy.

George Alper

Thanks to all who helped and supported or otherwise contributed to this project:
Tony Beram, Marty Fettman, John Reda, Bryan Steele, Mark Metzger, Mario Mendia, Pam and Greg Gerber, Jen Vizcarra, Jaye and Edward, Eric and Jake, Bob, and of course, Maryellen, Rowan Jeri, and Charley Rose - 1-4-3-∞.

Indian Neck Folk Festival May 6, 1961

Gerde's Folk City 11 West 4th St., Greenwich Village NY Sept. 26, 1961

Alper Family Household Jan. 1962

Watching TV

Alper Family Household Jan. 1962 with Suze Rotolo

Alper Family Household Jan. 1962 with Jackie Alper, Suze Rotolo and Guy McKenzie

With Suze and Lena Spencer (and Pasha)

Playing building blocks with George Alper in the Alper Family Household Jan. 13, 1962

Jeri Alper joins in

"We were at Lena's (Caffe Lena), and someone called and said this guy was at the bus station and needed a ride. Joe and I went down and picked him up and brought him to Saratoga. He needed a place to stay, so we offered to put him up. From that point on, for a few years, whenever he came to town Dylan would stay with us.
We didn't have any money, and neither did he. We would put a few coins or a dollar together, and I would go down to the store and get a few things to make supper. One night we made this casserole sorta thing, with a lot of filler and a little meat. I remember he liked my cooking, so I knew he was crazy. He would ask for that dish every time he came to visit."

-Jackie Alper

Alper Family Household Jan. 14, 1962

At Caffe Lena Jan. 14, 1962

Attic of the Alper Family Household Jan. 15, 1962

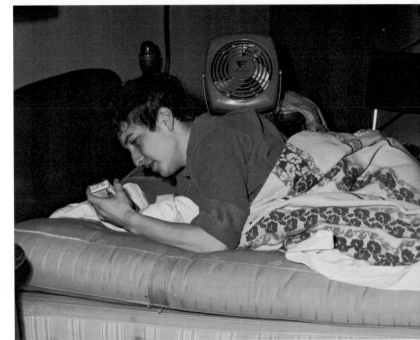

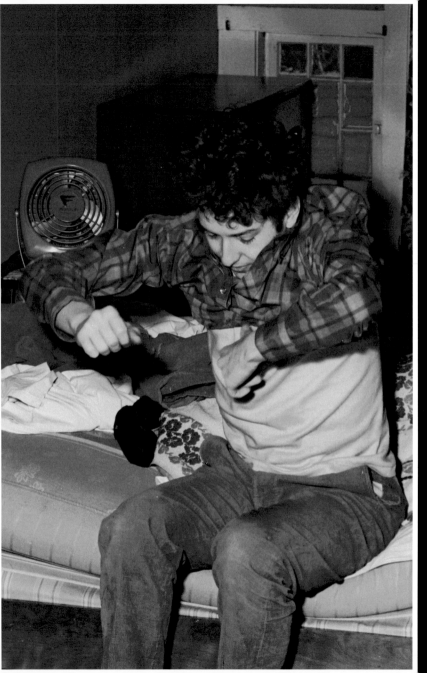

At the Alper family piano Jan. 15, 1962

Jaye Alper watches Dylan play piano

Browsing thru the album collection of Jackie and Joe Alper

Writing songs at the Alper household Jan. 1962

San Remo Coffeehouse, Schenectady, NY Jan. 1962

At the Alper Family Household, Schenectady, NY Jan. 1962

With Suze at the Alper Family Household

Freewheelin' recording sessions New York City Apr. 24, 1962 with unidentified techs and others

Producer John Hammond, Sr. talks to Dylan

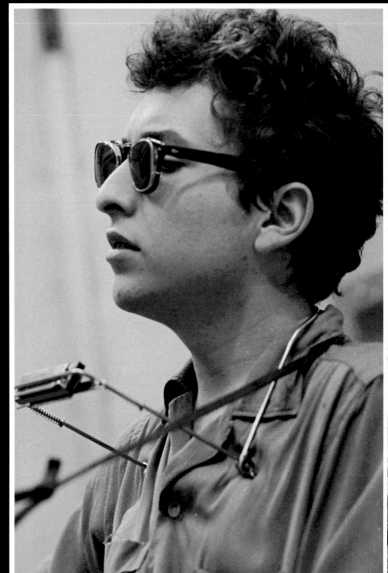

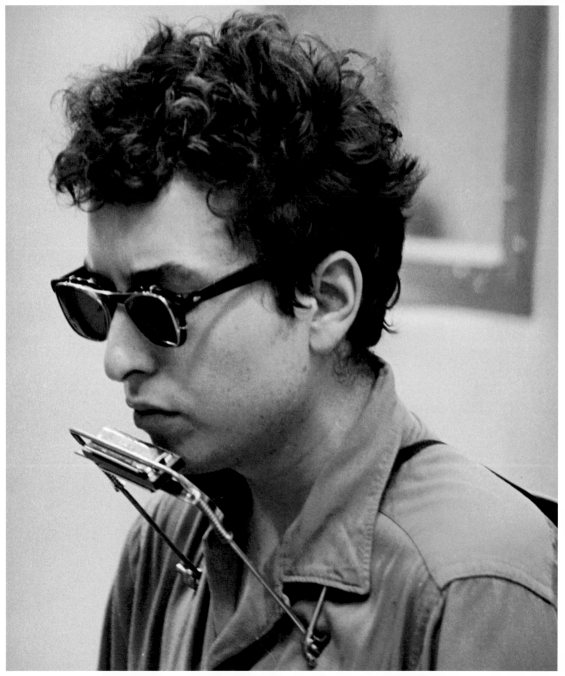

With John Hammond, Sr. , producer of *Freewheelin'*

Pete Seeger (sitting on floor) and others at Gil Turner's wedding

Rex, Gary Davis, Gil Turner, unidentified, Dylan, unidentified, unidentified, Mark Spoelstra, unidentified

Rev. Gary Davis sleeps thru a Dylan song as Gil Turner looks on

Newlyweds Gil and Lori Turner listen to a Dylan tune

Entrance to Newport Folk Festival, 1964

Len Chandler enjoys an impromptu Dylan set

On stage at Newport 1964

With Joan Baez on stage at Newport 1964

First electric performance at Newport 1965

First electric performance at Newport 1965

Acoustic performance at Newport 1965